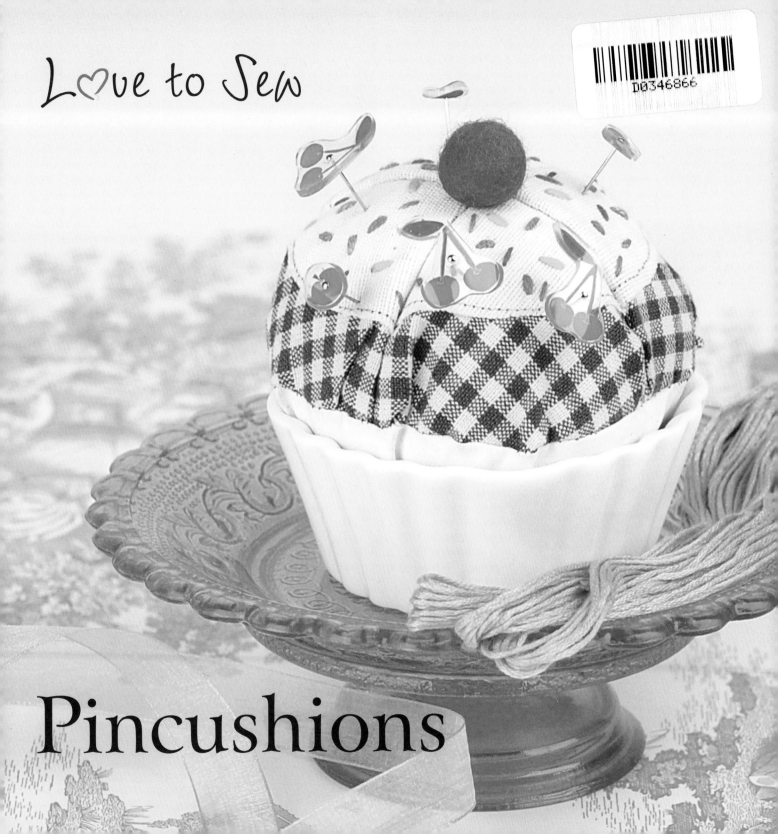

Love to Sew

Pincushions

Dedication

To Rod, the best four-legged
friend I ever had.

Love to Sew

Pincushions

Salli-Ann Cook

Search Press

First published in Great Britain 2012

Search Press Limited
Wellwood, North Farm Road,
Tunbridge Wells, Kent TN2 3DR

Text copyright © Salli-Ann Cook 2012

Photographs by Debbie Patterson at Search Press Studio

Photographs and design copyright © Search Press Ltd. 2012

ISBN: 978-1-84448-822-3

The Publishers and author can accept no responsibility for any consequences arising from the information, advice or instructions given in this publication.

Suppliers
If you have difficulty in obtaining any of the materials and equipment mentioned in this book, then please visit the Search Press website for details of suppliers: www.searchpress.com

You are invited to visit the author's website:
www.ticklyspider.co.uk

Acknowledgements

Huge thanks to Keith, Chloe, Syd, Gay, Mum, Dad, Mama-Fay, Em and Dan, Nick, Tula, Meatball and the rest of the Tribe. Without their support, encouragement and reassurance, this book would never have been completed.

Anne, for believing in me and being a great friend.

Roz Dace for plucking me from obscurity! Sophie Kersey, my editor, for having a little faith in my zany ideas and all at Search Press for putting this book together.

Thank you to Debbie Patterson, photographer extraordinaire, for making my little projects look wonderful and finally, thank you to all of my fabric suppliers, to Bronte Glen and everyone else who inadvertently helped to contribute to this book.

Printed in China

Draught Excluder, page 18

Mini Monster, page 20

Mini Garden, page 26

Hedgehog, page 28

Storm in a Teacup, page 34

Fried Egg, page 36

Cheese, page 46

Wristwatch, page 48

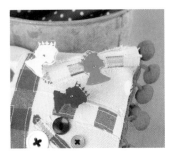

Union Jack Pillow, page 22

Cupcake, page 24

Contents

Christmas Pud, page 30

Halloween Pumpkin, page 32

Sunflower, page 38

Radio, page 40

Voodoo Doll, page 42

Flat Cat, page 44

Machine Heart, page 50

Magician's Hat, page 52

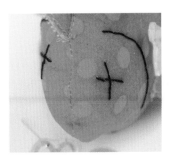

Fish, page 54

Home Sweet Home, page 56

Introduction

Pincushions have been around for centuries: the first recorded use of them is from the Tudor period in England. Before this, as metal pins and needles were expensive, they were stored in protective cases of bone or ivory. As they reduced in price over time, it became regular practice to use elaborate stuffed shapes to store them.

Pincushions were given more prestige in the Victorian period. As parlours became more lavish, collections of pincushions took pride of place on mantelpieces. Since then, they have grown in popularity, both for use and for avid collectors. One popular type is the *biscornu*, an eight-sided French pincushion, often heavily embroidered with intricate designs. The word literally means 'quirky'.

A pincushion is essential for anyone who sews, but who says it needs to be boring or humdrum? Surely something that you see often should be a splendid or humorous object that makes you smile, and why not something quirky like a voodoo doll or a fried egg?

In this book, I show how easy pincushions can be to make. There are twenty designs to choose from so there should be something for everyone, whether you are making it for yourself or for a friend who sews. Once you have mastered a few practicalities, the only constraint is your imagination.

How to make decorative pins

Draw the image on one side of some shrink plastic, roughly five times larger than the final size. Colour in with felt pens, paint pens or permanent markers. Cut out the image with sharp scissors, leaving a small border. Turn the image over and carefully push a stainless steel pin all the way through the middle so that the head just protrudes. Do not use pins with plastic heads. Preheat the oven to 160°C/320°F/gas mark 3. Put the pins on a non-stick baking tray and put in the oven for a few minutes. Once shrunk, remove from the oven and put on a heatproof board. After a few minutes, the shrink plastic will harden and set.

Materials & equipment

Before you begin your pincushion making, you need to assemble a few bits and pieces. You will have some of them around the house, but it is worth buying others, especially a good, sharp pair of fabric shears. All the pincushions can be made with a fairly basic sewing machine and small pieces of fabric.

Fabrics

I am lucky enough to have a huge stash of fabrics, amassed over the years. The beauty of pincushions, however, is that you can make them from small pieces of fabric, so you will be able to find a lot in markets or remnant bins. Another good source is charity shops. The best type of fabric for pincushions is heavyweight fabric such as calico, canvas or heavy cotton twill. These will stand up to lots of wear and tear, and they are nice to sew with and fray less. Lighter-weight fabrics such as polycotton or cotton mix are available in a much wider variety of colours or prints, but they tend to fray more. If you are using these, you can reinforce them with fusible web, which helps to prevent fraying. Cotton-mix fabrics contrast well with the calicos or cotton twills, so they are great for appliqué details. Shirts and dresses from charity shops are a good source of these fabrics. I have even been known to use tea towels for sewing projects if I like the print.

A selection of machine and embroidery threads.

Threads

You will need machine threads in a few basic colours to match your fabrics. In addition, embroidery threads are used for embroidered details and for decorating appliqué details. Strong thread is required for the Christmas Pud pincushion on page 30.

Opposite
A variety of heavyweight and lighter fabrics, ideal for making pincushions.

Sewing machine

The pincushions were made using a reasonably priced household sewing machine, with a few stitches to choose from and a two-step buttonhole function.

Embellishments

Buttons are used with many of the projects. I have also used pompom trims in red and white, and a red felt ball.

Other materials

Toy stuffing Great stuff for filling pincushions!

Fusible web This is good for appliqué pieces. It also helps to stiffen and reinforce more delicate fabrics, preventing them from fraying.

Sharp scissors You will need good fabric shears for cutting out the fabrics, paper or household scissors for paper items, and embroidery scissors for cutting threads.

Tape measure This is for general sewing use but also for measuring accessories like your teacup or plant pot so that you can make the pincushion to match.

Ruler For measuring and drawing straight lines.

Pencil or tailor's chalk For drawing on fabric to mark out patterns or details to be embroidered.

Tracing paper or greaseproof paper For tracing the templates from the book. Alternatively, you can just use the paper on to which you photocopy or scan and print them. Then cut them out.

Iron-on transfer paper This is used with a **permanent black pen** for putting on the eyes of the Mini Monster pincushion (page 20).

Sewing needles Use a hand sewing needle for hand closing. Choose a size you can work with comfortably; they are available in sizes 1–12. Use an embroidery needle for embroidery as these have a longer, wider eye to take embroidery thread. They are available in sizes 1–10, but choose whichever size suits you best. Darning needles are long thick needles with a large eye to accommodate thick yarns and threads. These again are available in various sizes. This needle is best to use for the overstitching of the Halloween Pumpkin pincushion (page 32) and any other job where you need to push the needle through several thicknesses of fabric or stuffing. It is generally a good idea to buy a pack of mixed needles, which are widely available from any haberdashery store.

Pins Vital unless you have more than one pair of hands!

Crochet hook For pushing stuffing into the far reaches of a pincushion.

Iron For attaching fusible web and iron-on tranfer paper, as well as for ironing the fabrics and pressing seams.

Accessories You will need a teacup and saucer for the Storm in a Teacup pincushion (page 34), a plant pot for the Mini Garden (page 26) and a ceramic cupcake case for the Cupcake pincushion (page 24).

Craft knife and cutting mat These are used for cutting buttonholes after stitching them using the sewing machine.

Paper punch For making the holes to go on the Cheese pincushion (page 46).

Shrink plastic and pens I used these to make the decorative pins (see page 6).

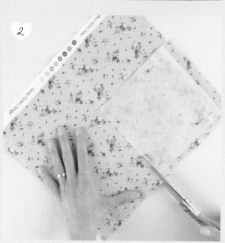

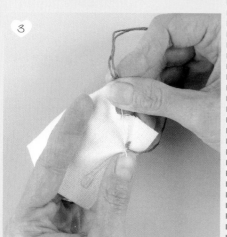

Basic techniques

All the basic techniques for the pincushions are shown through the making of this simple square pincushion. The templates for the pincushions are on pages 58–64. Note that when a project has asymmetrical templates, and you need to cut two pieces to place right sides outwards, if your fabric has a right and wrong side, you need to flip the template over to cut out the second piece.

Transferring the design

1 Draw the design, here a 14 x 14cm (5½ x 5½in) square, on baking parchment, and cut it out to make a template. All the templates are provided in this book, so you could also photocopy or scan and print it, then cut it out.

2 Pin the template to the main fabric and cut round it using fabric shears. Cut out two of the squares, for the front and back of the pincushion.

Embroidery

3 Cut out a piece of calico 6 x 6cm (2³⁄₈ x 2³⁄₈in). Draw the design, a needle shape, on the calico. Thread an embroidery needle with a full thickness of grey embroidery thread and back stitch along the design (see diagram right). Change to green thread to complete the embroidery.

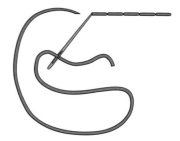

Back stitch

Using fusible web

Fusible web is used to attach one piece of fabric to another. It is also helpful in that it prevents fabric from fraying.

4 Cut a square of fusible web 6 x 6cm ($2^3/_8$ x $2^3/_8$in). Iron it on to the back of the embroidered calico piece. Iron a small piece of fusible web on to the back of some red fabric, then draw a heart shape on it freehand and cut it out. Peel off the backing from the heart and iron it on to the calico piece.

5 Peel the fusible web backing off the back of the calico piece with the embroidery and the heart on it.

6 Iron this piece on to one of your squares of main fabric.

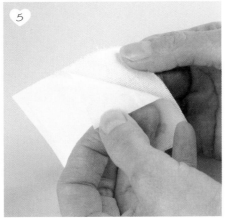

Machine appliqué

7 Thread up the sewing machine with matching thread in the top and beige in the bobbin. Set it to straight stitch and sew the decorated calico square to the main fabric.

Applying decorative effects

8 Thread an embroidery needle with a full thickness of black embroidery thread, and sew simple straight stitches around the edges of the central heart and around the square.

9 Choose coordinating buttons and sew these on down one side of the central square, still using the black embroidery thread.

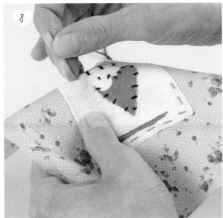

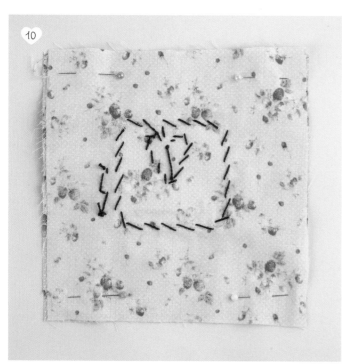

Sewing together

10 Place the front and back pieces of main fabric right sides together and pin them as shown.

11 With the sewing machine threaded up as before, sew the squares together, leaving a gap for stuffing, as follows: start two-thirds of the way along one side and sew to the edge, then continue all the way round the square, stopping a third of the way along the first side to leave your opening.

12 Turn the piece right sides out through the opening.

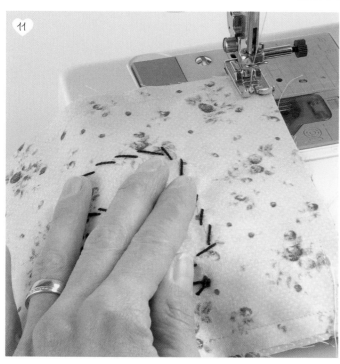

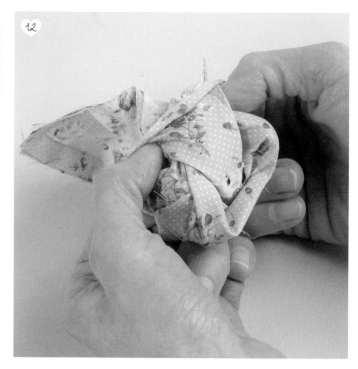

Stuffing and closing

13 Stuff the pincushion with toy stuffing, making sure you get the stuffing into all the corners.

14 Pin together the edges of the remaining opening.

15 Machine sew up the opening, going carefully over the pins.

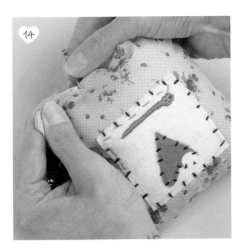

Projects

A pincushion is a small and accessible project that can be virtually any shape you like. With this in mind, I have dreamed up some quirky designs to put a new spin on a familiar object. The projects throughout this book are laid out in easy-to-follow steps so even the most inexperienced stitcher can master the art of making pincushions, and have fun doing it!

Draught Excluder

Materials

- red patterned fabric, 16 x 25cm (6¼ x 10in)
- cream fabric, 3 x 14cm (1¼ x 5½in)
- small coordinating buttons
- scraps of red patterned fabrics
- black embroidery thread
- fusible web
- toy stuffing

Tools

- fabric shears
- pins
- embroidery needle
- sewing machine and matching threads
- iron
- crochet hook

1 Cut the red patterned fabric in half so that you have two rectangles measuring 8 x 25cm (3⅛ x 10in).

2 Back the cream fabric and the scraps with fusible web.

3 Cut out four small hand-drawn hearts from the scraps of fabric. Remove the backing from the fusible web and pin the hearts on to the cream rectangle, equal distances apart.

4 Use black embroidery thread to sew these hearts in place using small stitches.

5 Remove the backing from the fusible web on the cream rectangle and iron it in the centre of one of the rectangles of red patterned fabric.

6 Machine stitch around the outside of the cream rectangle to stitch it in place, using red thread.

7 Use the black embroidery thread to sew four buttons at the right-hand end of the cream rectangle and one button at the other end.

8 Pin the two large rectangles together, right sides facing, and machine sew around both of the long sides and one of the shorter sides, leaving a 1cm (⅜in) seam allowance. Turn right sides out.

9 Stuff firmly with toy stuffing. You may need to use a crochet hook to reach the bottom end of the draught excluder.

10 Turn in the ends of the opening by 0.5cm (¼in) and pin. Machine stitch to close.

Templates for the eyes and tooth

Mini Monster

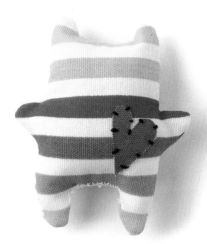

Materials

- ♥ striped fabric, 20 x 24cm (8 x 9½in)
- ♥ printable iron-on transfer paper for dark fabric
- ♥ toy stuffing
- ♥ scrap of red fabric
- ♥ tracing paper or greaseproof paper
- ♥ black embroidery thread

Tools

- ♥ fabric shears and paper scissors
- ♥ tailor's chalk or pencil
- ♥ iron
- ♥ sewing machine and matching threads
- ♥ pins
- ♥ embroidery needle
- ♥ crochet hook
- ♥ hand sewing needle

1 Scan or photocopy the eyes and tooth from this page on to printable white iron-on transfer paper and cut them out.

2 Cut out two monster shapes (see page 58) from the striped fabric and a heart from the scrap of red fabric.

3 Place the eyes on the front of one of the monster pieces and cover with the tracing or greaseproof paper. Iron them in place, holding the iron over them for one or two minutes to ensure that the image is transferred.

4 Use tailor's chalk or pencil to mark on a big smile. Thread up the sewing machine with red thread and use a very close zigzag stitch to sew on the smile. Change to white thread and sew on the tooth using straight stitch.

5 Hand sew the red heart to the bottom of the back piece of the monster using black embroidery thread in an embroidery needle and small stitches.

6 Pin the monster pieces right sides together and machine sew round the outside edge leaving a 5mm (¼in) seam allowance. Leave an opening for stuffing.

7 Snip into the seam allowance at 1cm (³⁄₈in) intervals, making sure you do not snip the seam.

8 Turn the monster the right way out and stuff firmly with toy stuffing. You may need a crochet hook to help you stuff right to the ends. Hand sew the opening closed.

Union Jack Pillow

Materials

- red gingham fabric, 20 x 30cm (8 x 12in)
- white cotton fabric, 13 x 16cm (5⅛ x 6¼in)
- blue spotted fabric, 15 x 15cm (6 x 6in)
- red pompom ribbon
- toy stuffing
- fusible web
- black embroidery thread
- white, red and blue buttons

Tools

- iron
- fabric shears
- sewing machine and matching threads
- embroidery needle
- pins
- hand sewing needle

1 Back the red gingham and blue spotted fabric with fusible web. Cut out a rectangle, 13 x 16cm (5 x 6¼in) from red gingham for the back of the pincushion. Photocopy all the templates (see page 58) and use them to cut out all the fabric pieces for appliqué. Peel off the backing from the fusible web and arrange the appliqué pieces on the white rectangle. Start with the red gingham cross in the centre and build up the pattern, leaving narrow white spaces between the pieces. When you are happy with the placing, iron them on.

2 Thread up the machine with white thread and stitch round the edges of all the appliqué pieces to secure them firmly.

3 Sew on the buttons using the black embroidery thread.

4 Place the appliquéd flag piece and the bottom red gingham piece right sides together. Cut the pompom ribbon to the length of the shorter sides and pin into place as shown, ensuring that the pompoms are on the inside of the pincushion.

5 Pin the gingham backing piece in place, making sure the ribbon strip is sandwiched firmly between the two sides of the pincushion.

6 Machine stitch all round three sides of the pincushion and half of the fourth side, leaving the rest open. Allow a 1cm (³⁄₈in) seam allowance.

7 Turn the pincushion right sides out and stuff firmly with toy stuffing. Pin the opening and use white thread to hand stitch it closed.

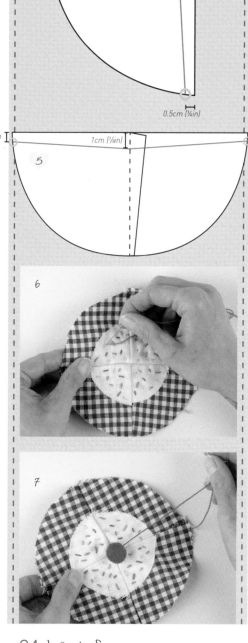

Cupcake

Materials

- brown gingham fabric, 20 x 20cm (8 x 8in)
- white fabric 30 x 30 (11¾ x 11¾in)
- red felt ball
- coloured embroidery thread
- fusible web
- toy stuffing
- ceramic cupcake case

Tools

- iron
- fabric shears
- embroidery needle
- ruler
- pencil
- sewing machine and matching threads
- hand sewing needle

1 Cut out two circles, one from the brown gingham fabric and one from the white, twice the diameter of your cupcake case. Back the remaining white fabric with fusible web and cut a second circle from it the same diameter as your cupcake case.

2 Remove the backing from the small white circle, place it in the centre of the gingham circle and iron it in place.

3 Fold the whole circle into equal quarters and run your fingers along the edges to crease them. Unfold and cut along the creases so that you have four equal-sized pieces.

4 Take two of the adjacent pieces and place them right sides together. Mark with a pencil and ruler 0.5cm (¼in) from the upright straight edge at the rounded outside edge and 1cm (³⁄₈in) from the upright straight edge on the horizontal straight edge (see diagram). Join these two marks together. Machine sew along the line you have marked. Repeat this process with the other two pieces.

5 You now have two semicircles. Place them right sides together and, as before, mark 0.5cm (¼in) from the rounded edge to 1cm (³⁄₈in) from the central point on both sides. Machine sew along the lines. This will form the slight dome of the cupcake.

6 Mark a few small random lines on the white part of the cupcake with pencil to resemble sprinkles. Hand sew these marks with embroidery threads in various colours, using simple straight stitch.

7 Using red embroidery thread, sew the red felt ball on to the centre of the cupcake.

8 Pin the large plain white circle over the right side of the pincushion and machine sew around three-quarters of the circle. Note that the doming process in steps 4 and 5 makes the top of the pincushion smaller than the white base, but this will not matter once you have sewn the parts together and turned them right sides out, as the excess will be inside.

9 Turn the right way out and stuff firmly with toy stuffing.

10 Using small hand stitches, sew the gap to close. Place the cupcake in your case.

Templates

Mini Garden

Materials

- small terracotta plant pot up to 10cm (4in) in diameter
- green fabric, 30 x 15cm (11¾ x 6in)
- white fabric, 15 x 20cm (6 x 8in)
- yellow fabric, 10 x 10cm (4 x 4in)
- green gingham fabric, 15 x 15cm (6 x 6in)
- fusible web

Tools

- fabric shears
- iron
- pins
- sewing machine and matching threads
- hand sewing needle

1 Cut two circles from the green fabric with a diameter one and a half times that of your plant pot. With the seam allowance, this should make a pincushion that sits neatly inside the rim.

2 Cut the white fabric in half lengthways. Fuse the two pieces together, right sides out, using fusible web. Repeat with the green gingham.

3 Cut four flower shapes from the bonded white fabric (see above) and three leaves from the gingham.

4 Iron fusible web to the back of the yellow fabric and cut out four flower centres.

5 Iron a yellow centre on to each white flower.

6 Pin the leaf shapes in place on one of the large green circles, then machine stitch the point of each one to fix it. Pin the flowers in place on top as shown.

7 Machine stitch around the centres in yellow and the flowers in white to fix them in place. Machine stitch around the leaves in dark green to decorate them.

8 With all the appliqué in place, pin the decorated circle to the other green circle, right sides together. Fold the protruding leaves inside as you pin.

9 Machine sew around the outside of the circles, leaving a seam allowance of 1cm (⅜in). Leave a gap of 2cm (¾in).

10 Carefully snip into the edge of the circles at 1cm (⅜in) intervals, making sure you do not cut through the seam.

11 Turn right sides out and stuff firmly with toy stuffing. Pin the opening closed and hand sew to close it with small stitches. Place the pincushion in your plant pot, with stuffing or paper underneath to support it, if necessary.

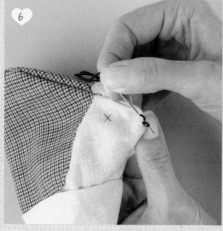

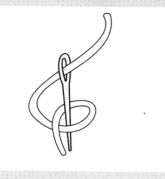

French knot diagram.

Hedgehog

Materials

- ♥ Beige fabric, 30 x 30cm (11¾ x 11¾in)
- ♥ brown checked fabric, 15 x 20cm (6x 8in)
- ♥ fusible web
- ♥ black embroidery thread
- ♥ small black button
- ♥ toy stuffing

Tools

- ♥ fabric shears
- ♥ iron
- ♥ sewing machine and matching threads
- ♥ pins
- ♥ embroidery needle
- ♥ pencil
- ♥ hand sewing needle

1 Back the checked pieces with fusible web. Using the templates on pages 58 and 59, cut out two large side pieces and one base piece from beige fabric and two smaller side pieces from brown checked fabric. If your fabrics have a right and a wrong side, make sure you turn the templates over to cut out the second beige and checked side pieces.

2 Place the checked pieces on the larger beige pieces of the hedgehog shape and iron them on. Machine sew around the edge of the appliqué in beige thead.

3 Pin both sides of the hedgehog right sides together and machine sew from the nose end to the tail end.

4 While the hedgehog is still inside out, pin the the beige base piece in place along one edge of the bottom, making sure that the right side faces inwards. Machine sew.

5 Turn the hedgehog right sides out and use a pencil to mark the position of the nose and eyes.

6 Using black embroidery thread and an embroidery needle, sew a small cross for one eye and a French knot for the nose (see diagram). Sew on the button for the other eye.

7 Stuff the hedgehog firmly with toy stuffing and hand sew with a simple back stitch in beige thread to close the remaining open side.

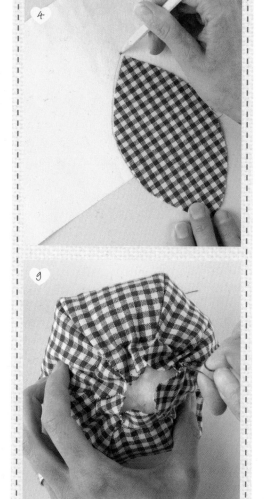

Christmas Pud

Materials

- brown gingham fabric, 50 x 50cm (19¾ x 19¾in)
- green fabric, 20 x 20cm (8 x 8in)
- white fabric, 30 x 30cm (11¾ x 11¾in)
- fusible web
- red felt ball
- toy stuffing
- 3 white and 2 green buttons
- 1 large brown button
- cream and green embroidery thread
- strong brown thread

Tools

- fabric shears
- iron
- sewing machine and matching threads
- pins
- pencil
- embroidery needle

1 Using the template on page 60, cut out six pieces for the main body of the pudding from the gingham. Back the white fabric and the green fabric with fusible web.

2 Cut the green fabric in half and iron the two pieces together with fusible web. Cut two holly leaves from the bonded fabric using the template on page 60.

3 Thread up the machine with dark green thread and sew around the edges of the holly leaves and up the middle of each one. Place them end to end, overlapping by 5mm (¼in) and sew them together.

4 Place one pudding piece half over the edge of the white fabric. Use a pencil to mark around the piece and remove it. Do this for all six pudding pieces, and cut the white pieces out. These will make the white sauce on top of the pudding.

5 Draw a wavy line at the bottom of each white piece to suggest dripping sauce, and cut along the wavy lines.

6 Remove the backing from the white sauce pieces and iron them on to the gingham pudding pieces.

7 Begin sewing all the pudding pieces together lengthways. Place two pieces right sides together, pin in place, and machine sew from the top of one edge to 2cm (¾in) before the bottom, leaving a 5mm (¼in) seam allowance. Repeat to sew together the whole pudding, sewing the edge of the final piece to the edge of the first piece. Turn right sides out.

8 Use a zigzag stitch to sew the joined part of the holly leaves to the centre of the pudding top. Use an embroidery needle to hand stitch the red felt ball on top and the white and green buttons on the side. Stuff the pudding with toy stuffing.

9 Using strong brown thread, hand sew running stitch all round the bottom of the pudding where the machine stitching ends. Pull firmly to gather up the pudding and oversew to close. Sew on a large button to conceal the closure.

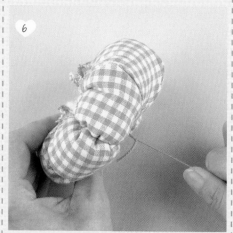

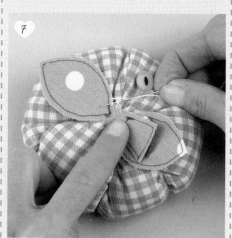

Halloween Pumpkin

Materials

- orange gingham, 50 x 50cm (19¾ x 19¾in)
- green fabric, 20 x 20cm (8 x 8in)
- orange embroidery thread
- toy stuffing
- fusible web
- orange buttons

Tools

- fabric shears
- iron
- pins
- sewing machine and matching threads
- darning needle

1 Use the templates on page 60 to cut out six pumpkin pieces from orange gingham, plus four leaf and two stalk pieces from green fabric. Back the leaf and stalk pieces with fusible web.

2 Remove the backing from two leaf shapes, place them back to back and iron them together. Do the same with the two stalk pieces, then place two more leaf pieces back to back, sandwich the end of the stalk between them and iron them together, trapping the stalk. Machine stitch around the edges of the leaves and stalk with dark green thread.

3 Construct your pumpkin by sewing the eye-shaped pieces together side by side, lengthwise (see step 7 of the Christmas Pud, page 30). Leave a 5mm (¼in) seam allowance and leave the top 2cm (¾in) open.

4 Thread a darning needle with a long length of orange embroidery thread and knot one end firmly. Push the needle up through the bottom of the pumpkin where all the pieces meet and out of the top opening. Keeping the thread in place, stuff the pumpkin firmly with toy stuffing.

5 Take the still attached needle and sew round the opening at the top of the pumpkin with running stitch, and pull tight to gather. Knot the thread firmly but do not cut it.

6 Bring the thread down over the side of the pumpkin where two pieces meet, then push the needle up through the bottom of the pumpkin and come out of the top again. Pull tightly. Repeat five times until you have gone right round the pumpkin, then secure the thread at the top.

7 Sew on a button at the centre of the bottom of the pumpkin to neaten, and more buttons on to the top of the pumpkin to decorate. Sew the leaves and stalk on to the top with small back stitches.

Storm in a Teacup

Materials

♥ beige fabric twice as wide all round as the teacup diameter
♥ patterned grey fabric, 15 x 15cm (6 x 6in)
♥ grey fabric, 15 x 15 (6 x 6in)
♥ yellow fabric, 10 x 20cm (4 x 8in)
♥ brown embroidery thread
♥ fusible web
♥ toy stuffing
♥ teacup and saucer

Tools

♥ pencil or tailor's chalk
♥ fabric shears
♥ iron
♥ ruler
♥ sewing machine and matching threads
♥ embroidery needle
♥ pins

1 Cut the yellow fabric in half and fuse the two pieces together with fusible web. Using the template on page 60, cut out three or four lightning bolts. Machine stitch round each one using matching thread.

2 Bond the grey fabric to the patterened grey fabric using fusible web. Cut out two clouds, using the template on page 60, and machine stitch round each one with black thread.

3 Measure the diameter of your teacup, as shown, and multiply the measurement by two. Cut out a circle of this diameter from the beige fabric.

4 Use a pencil or tailor's chalk to mark the centre of the beige circle and the circumference of the teacup round this. Draw a spiral that runs from the centre to the edge of the circle. Stitch the spiral in brown embroidery thread using back stitch and starting in the centre.

5 Referring to the photograph, pin the clouds and lightning bolts to the spiral. Attach the clouds with grey thread and the lightning bolts with yellow thread, leaving most of the shapes unattached for a three-dimensional effect. This can be done by machine, as shown, stitching over the previous machine stitches, or by hand.

6 Using a double length of beige thread, work running stitch round the beige circle about 1.5cm (⅝in) from the edge, so you can gather it up. Do not fasten off the thread yet.

7 Form a ball of toy stuffing to fill the pincushion and place it in the centre of the beige circle on the wrong side. Pull up the gathering thread tightly and secure it with a knot. Place the ball in your teacup.

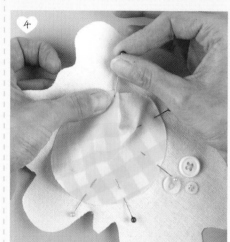

Fried Egg

Materials

- ♥ white fabric, 20 x 40cm (8 x 15¾in)
- ♥ yellow gingham, 15 x 15cm (6 x 6in)
- ♥ fusible web
- ♥ toy stuffing
- ♥ white or clear buttons
- ♥ yellow embroidery thread

Tools

- ♥ fabric shears
- ♥ iron
- ♥ sewing machine and matching threads
- ♥ pins
- ♥ embroidery needle

1 Use the template on page 61 to cut out two egg shapes from the white fabric. If your white fabric has a right and wrong side, remember to turn the template over to draw one of the shapes. Back one egg shape with fusible web. Cut out a circle 9cm (3½in) in diameter from the yellow gingham and back this with fusible web.

2 Sew the buttons in place on the top egg shape with the yellow embroidery thread.

3 Fix together the two white pieces by removing the backing from the fusible web and ironing, then machine stitch round the edges with white thread and straight stitch.

4 Pin the yolk circle in place, making a pleat in the circle to create the domed shape.

5 Machine sew around the yolk as close to the edge as possible using yellow thread and straight stitch, and leaving a gap of 1.5cm (⅝in) for stuffing. Stiff firmly with toy stuffing, then pin the opening closed.

6 Machine sew the opening closed. Sew round the yolk again for decoration using white thread, then sew round the edges of the egg white using yellow thread and zigzag stitch.

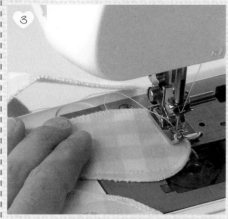

Sunflower

Materials

- ♥ yellow gingham fabric, 60 x 60cm (23½ x 23½in)
- ♥ brown gingham fabric, 30 x 30cm (11¾ x 11¾in)
- ♥ beige fabric, 20 x 20cm (8x 8in)
- ♥ fusible web
- ♥ greaseproof paper or tracing paper
- ♥ toy stuffing
- ♥ brown buttons
- ♥ black embroidery thread

Tools

- ♥ pencil
- ♥ fabric shears
- ♥ iron
- ♥ embroidery needle
- ♥ sewing machine and matching threads
- ♥ pins

1 Transfer the template on page 62 on to greaseproof or tracing paper four times to make the complete sunflower shape. Cut out two whole sunflowers from yellow gingham, as well as one 11cm (4⅜in) diameter circle and one 10cm (4in) diameter circle from brown gingham. From the beige fabric, cut one 11cm (4⅜in) diameter circle.

2 Back all the fabric pieces with fusible web. Sew buttons on to one of the yellow pieces using black embroidery thread. Peel off the backing from the fusible web on the two yellow flowers and iron them together, right sides out.

3 Thread up the machine with yellow thread and sew round the edges of the yellow flower using straight stitch.

4 Remove the backing from the fusible web on the large brown gingham circle, and iron this on to the back of the sunflower. Do the same for the beige circle and iron this on to the front. Machine sew around the edge of the beige circle in dark brown thread.

5 Pin the smaller brown gingham circle on to the centre of the sunflower, making two pleats opposite each other to create a domed shape. Machine sew round the edge using dark brown thread and leaving a gap of around 2cm (¾in) for stuffing.

6 Stuff the dome with toy stuffing, pin the opening closed and then machine sew to close.

7 Change to zigzag stitch and machine sew round the edge of the dome again for decorative effect, and to hide any untidy stitching.

The template for the dial.

French knot diagram.

Radio

Materials

- dark grey fabric, 45 x 45cm (17¾ x 17¾in)
- black fabric, 10 x 5cm (4 x 2in)
- white fabric, 5 x 5cm (2 x 2in)
- gold, black and red embroidery threads
- fusible web
- toy stuffing

Tools

- fabric shears
- pencil or tailor's chalk
- iron
- embroidery needle
- sewing machine and matching threads
- pins
- hand sewing needle

1 Cut out four rectangles, 12 x 6cm (4¾ x 2⅜in), and two squares, 6 x 6cm (2⅜ x 2⅜in), from the grey fabric for the body of the radio. To make the appliqué pieces, cut out two 3.5cm (1⅜in) diameter circles from black fabric for speakers and a use the template above to make the dial shape from white fabric. Back all the appliqué pieces with fusible web.

2 Remove the backing from the fusible web and iron the appliqué pieces in place on one of the grey rectangles, to create the radio front with speakers and a dial.

3 Embroider the dial and arrow using red and black embroidery thread. Machine stitch grids on the speaker pieces using light grey thread.

4 Stitch three French knots in gold embroidery thread (see diagram), to make the radio's knobs.

5 Pin all the long sides of the radio pieces together, with right sides facing inwards, and machine sew them with black thread to create a hollow box shape.

6 Pin and stitch one of the end pieces into place. Pin on the other end piece and machine sew around three of the sides, leaving one open.

7 Turn right sides out. Carefully machine stitch close to each machined edge of the radio. This will add stability and make the radio look more box-shaped.

8 Stuff the radio with toy stuffing, taking care to fill it completely without making the sides bulge too much.

9 Close the final side by hand using a small back stitch and black thread.

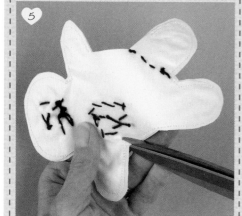

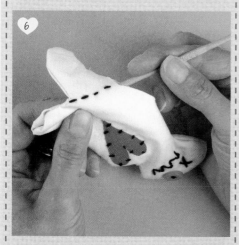

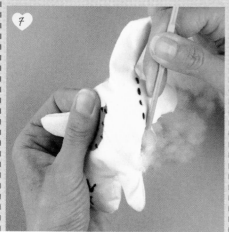

Voodoo Doll

Materials

- ♥ cream fabric, 40 x 40cm (15¾ x 15¾in)
- ♥ scrap of red fabric
- ♥ 1 button
- ♥ black embroidery thread
- ♥ fusible web
- ♥ toy stuffing

Tools

- ♥ iron
- ♥ fabric shears
- ♥ pencil or tailor's chalk
- ♥ embroidery needle
- ♥ hand sewing needle
- ♥ pins
- ♥ sewing machine and matching threads
- ♥ crochet hook

1 Back the fabrics with fusible web, then transfer the template on page 63 and cut out two body pieces in cream fabric and a heart from the scrap of red.

2 Use a pencil or tailor's chalk to draw on a large X for one eye and a zigzag mouth.

3 Remove the backing from the heart and iron it in place. Hand sew small stitches around the edge with black embroidery thread. Embroider the X for the eye, the zigzag mouth and a line of stitches between the body and one leg. Sew on a button for the other eye.

4 Pin the two body pieces right sides together. Machine sew around the edge using white thread, leaving a 5mm (¼in) seam allowance, and a 2cm (¾in) gap in the side between an arm and a leg for turning out and stuffing.

5 To keep the curves smooth when the doll is turned out, leave it inside out and carefully snip all the way round, almost up to the stitching, at 5mm (¼in) intervals, making sure you do not cut into the seams.

6 Turn the doll right sides out through the gap. You might need a crochet hook to poke out his extremities!

7 Stuff firmly with toy stuffing, using the crochet hook again to push it into any tricky areas. Close the remaining gap with small hand stitches in white thread.

French knot diagram.

Flat Cat

Materials

- grey checked fabric, 25 x 30cm (10 x 12in)
- white fabric, 10 x 10cm (4 x 4in)
- scraps of pink fabric
- black embroidery thread
- button
- fusible web
- toy stuffing

Tools

- fabric shears
- iron
- sewing machine and matching threads
- embroidery needle
- crochet hook
- pins

1 Back all the fabrics with fusible web. Fold the grey fabric in half and cut out the cat through both layers using the template on page 64. Cut a tummy shape from the white fabric using the template. Draw paw and nose shapes freehand on the pink fabric scraps and cut them out.

2 Iron the paws, nose and white tummy on to one cat piece. Machine sew around each piece with white thread to fix firmly.

3 Use pencil or tailor's chalk to draw on the cross eye and the position of the whiskers. Embroider a cross stitch with black embroidery thread and sew on a button for the other eye. Embroider a row of three French knots (see diagram) on either side of the face for whiskers, leaving a tail of thread from each one. Trim to about 1.5cm (^{5}/$_8$in).

4 Pin the front and back of the cat together with the right sides facing outwards. Carefully machine sew around the edge of the tail using black thread.

5 Remove the pins and use a small amount of toy stuffing to stuff the tail. Use a crochet hook to push the stuffing down.

6 Pin the front and back together again and machine sew around the edge, leaving a gap of 2cm (¾in) for stuffing.

7 Stuff the rest of the cat, again using the crochet hook to help push down the stuffing. Pin and then machine sew the gap to close.

The template for the end of the cheese.

Cheese

Materials

- yellow fabric, 25 x 30cm (9⅞ x 11¾in)
- black fabric, 15 x 15cm (6 x 6in)
- fusible web
- toy stuffing

Tools

- iron
- hole punch
- pins
- sewing machine and matching threads
- hand sewing needle

The template for the cheese segment.

1 Back the black fabric with fusible web and on the underside draw circles for the holes in the cheese. Cut them out. For smaller holes, use a hole punch.

2 Use the templates to cut out two segments, one curved end shape and two 12 x 5cm (4¾x 2in) rectangles from the yellow fabric. Remove the backing from the black hole pieces, place them randomly on the right sides of the yellow pieces and iron to fix.

3 Pin the top segment to one of the long rectangles with right sides facing. Machine sew with matching thread. Repeat to pin and sew on the other long rectangle.

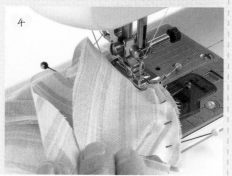

4 The long rectangles should meet at the point of the segment piece. Pin these right sides together and machine sew them. Pin the curved end piece into place and carefully machine stitch along the top and sides, leaving the bottom open for stuffing.

5 Pin the bottom segment in place with right sides facing and machine sew, still leaving the curved end open.

6 Turn the cheese right sides out and stuff firmly with toy stuffing. If you do this carefully, you can form a curve at the end of the cheese.

7 Pin the final curved shape in place and hand sew to close it.

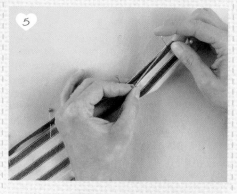

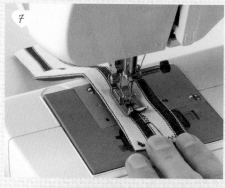

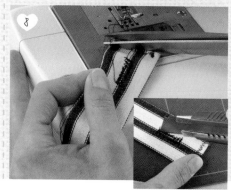

Wristwatch

Materials

- black fabric, 45 x 45cm (17¾ x 17¾in)
- cream fabric, 10 x 10cm (4 x 4in)
- gold and black embroidery thread
- 3 buttons
- striped fabric, 20 x 40cm (8 x 15¾in)

Tools

- tape measure
- fabric shears
- pencil or tailor's chalk
- embroidery needle
- sewing machine and matching threads
- pins
- craft knife and cutting mat
- hand sewing needle

1 Use a tape measure to measure the circumference of your wrist. Cut out a 9cm (3½in) diameter circle and a rectangle 29 x 5cm (11½ x 2in) from black fabric for the back and sides of the wristwatch, and a 9cm (3½in) diameter circle from cream fabric for the front.

2 The strap needs to be 5cm (2in) wide and the length should be the circumference of your wrist plus 3cm (1¼in). Cut it from the striped fabric, with the stripes lengthways.

3 Using a pencil or tailor's chalk, draw a watch face on the right side of the cream fabric, with a 12, 3, 6 and 9 and watch hands. Embroider the numbers and the centre of the watch face in black, then embroider the hands in gold thread.

4 Pin the long rectangle of black fabric to the watch face, right sides together. Machine sew them together with black thread. Leave the short ends of the long strip unsewn.

5 Fold over the long edges of the watch strap piece by 5mm (¼in) and pin them, then fold the strap in half lengthways and pin in place.

6 Machine sew along the long edge using black thread and straight stitch. Sew along the short edges using zigzag stitch.

7 Work out where your watch will go in the middle of the strap, then make three marks for the position of the buttonholes on one end of the strap. Follow your sewing machine guidelines to make the buttonholes. My machine has a two-step buttonhole. The first step shown is the stitching to reinforce the buttonhole.

8 Remove from the machine and snip the threads. Place the strap on a cutting mat and use a craft knife to cut the buttonholes.

9 Sew buttons on the other end of the strap. Place the strap over the remaining black circle of watch fabric, so that the circle is where the watch will be. Pin in place. Machine sew in a square formation on the strap to attach it to the circle.

10 Fold the strap inwards and secure it with pins so it does not overlap the circle edges. Take the inside-out watch face and sides and pin the sides to the black base, with the strap inside the pinned circle. Machine sew carefully around the pinned circle.

11 Turn the watch right sides out, stuff it and hand stitch the opening closed.

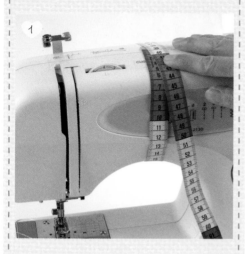

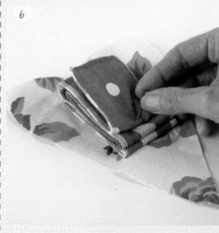

Machine Heart

Materials

- ♥ pink patterned fabric, 20 x 30cm (8 x 11¾in)
- ♥ red gingham, 50 x 8cm (17¾ x 8in)
- ♥ spotted red fabric, 50 x 8cm (19¾ x 3in)
- ♥ white pompom trim
- ♥ large red button

Tools

- ♥ fabric shears
- ♥ tape measure
- ♥ pencil or tailor's chalk
- ♥ sewing machine and matching threads
- ♥ pins
- ♥ craft knife and cutting mat
- ♥ Hand sewing needle

1 Cut out two hearts from the pink fabric (see page 62). To find the length of the strap, measure the area of the sewing machine where you will attach the pincushion. Add 10cm (4in) to this length and make the width 6cm (2⅜in). Cut one of these rectangles from spotted fabric and one from gingham.

2 Sew the button to one end of the gingham piece and machine a buttonhole (see page 48) at the end of the spotted piece, ensuring that the strap will fit snugly to your machine.

3 Pin the strap pieces right sides together with the buttonhole at one end and the button at the other, and machine sew round the edges, leaving one short end open.

4 Turn the strap right sides out and machine sew the open end to close it.

5 Place the strap, spotted side up, with the middle point on top of the right side of one of the heart shapes, so that the strap runs lengthwise down the heart. Attach by machine sewing a small square through the strap and heart.

6 Concertina fold the strap on to itself, making sure none of it overlaps the heart shape and pin to secure.

7 Pin the pompom trim into place between the two hearts with right sides facing and the pompoms pointing towards the inside.

8 Carefully machine sew around the whole heart shape, remembering to leave a gap of 4cm (1½in) for turning out.

9 Turn the right way out and stuff the heart firmly.

10 Close the opening with small hand stitches.

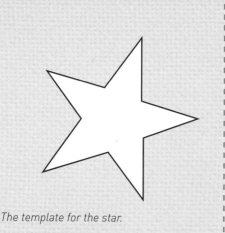

The template for the star.

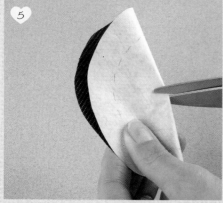

Magician's Hat

Materials

- ♥ dark grey fabric, 30 x 40cm (11¾ x 15¾in)
- ♥ black fabric, 10 x 10cm (4 x 4in)
- ♥ card 9 x 9cm (3½ x 3½in)
- ♥ scrap of yellow fabric
- ♥ grey ribbon
- ♥ fusible web
- ♥ toy stuffing

Tools

- ♥ fabric shears
- ♥ iron
- ♥ sewing machine and matching threads
- ♥ pins
- ♥ pencil
- ♥ hand sewing needle

1 Back the yellow, black and grey fabric with fusible web and cut out all the pieces as follows: one grey circle 7cm (2¾in) in diameter, one black circle the same size, and two grey circles 10cm (4in) in diameter, one grey rectangle 8 x 22cm (3⅛ x 8⅝in) and a star from the yellow fabric (see template above left).

2 Iron the yellow star on to the centre of the black circle. Machine sew around it with yellow thread to fix it.

3 Iron the black circle with the star centrally on to one of the larger grey circles.

4 Take the rectangle and pin the short ends together to form a cylinder, right sides together. Machine sew them together using black thread. Turn through.

5 Take the second large grey circle and mark a circle on the reverse just a little smaller than the circumference of the cylinder you made in step 4. Fold the circle in two and snip the centre to begin a hole, then cut out the inner circle as marked, to create a ring.

6 With the ring grey side up, place the cylinder through the hole. Snip into the cylinder at that end by 5mm (¼in) all the way round at 2cm (¾in) intervals.

7 Now fix the cylinder to the underside of the brim by first pinning the flaps made in step 6 into place and machine stitching to secure.

8 Iron the large grey circle with the black circle and star on it on to the underside of the hat brim. This creates the underside of the hat, where rabbits are pulled from, or where the hat goes on your head for the more conventional!

9 Stuff the cylinder of the hat firmly with toy stuffing.

10 Cut a circle of card a little smaller than the remaining small grey circle and push this into the open end of the hat, to stiffen the top. Pin and then hand sew the remaining grey circle in place to create the top of the hat.

11 Tie or sew the grey ribbon near to the brim to decorate.

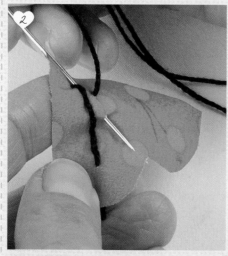

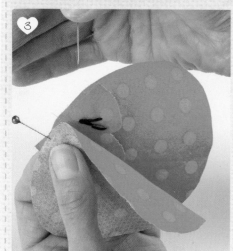

Fish

Materials

- ♥ pink spotty fabric, 40 x 40cm (15¾ x 15¾in)
- ♥ black embroidery thread
- ♥ fusible web
- ♥ toy stuffing

Tools

- ♥ iron
- ♥ fabric shears
- ♥ pencil or tailor's chalk
- ♥ pins
- ♥ sewing machine and matching threads
- ♥ embroidery needle
- ♥ hand sewing needle

1 Back the fabric with fusible web. Fold the fabric in half and cut the following through both layers: one body, one dorsal fin, one tail and two side fins, using the templates on pages 63 and 64.

2 Using pencil or tailor's chalk, mark the details on the fins, tail and face. Embroider with black thread using back stitch. Fuse together the two sides of the fins, dorsal fins and tail.

3 Pin and machine sew a side fin in position on the right side of each body piece. Put the two body pieces right sides together. Place the dorsal fin in position on the inside of the body. Do the same for the tail and pin into place.

4 Machine sew around the top half of the fish from the mouth to the tail end using matching thread.

5 Pin the belly piece of the fish in place. Push in the fins to make sure they are on the inside of the fish's body (while it is inside out). Machine sew along one side and two-thirds of the way along the other side, leaving a gap for turning out. Be careful not to catch the tail or fins in the stitches.

6 Carefully snip around the curves at 1cm (⅜in) intervals, taking care not to cut the seams. Turn the fish right sides out and stuff with toy stuffing.

7 Pin together the opening and hand sew to close.

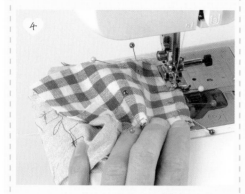

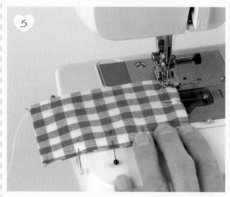

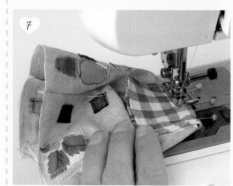

Home Sweet Home

Materials

- pale blue fabric, 45 x 45cm (17¾ x 17¾in)
- blue gingham fabric, 40 x 40cm (15¾ x 15¾in)
- scraps of fabric for appliqué
- fusible web
- toy stuffing

Tools

- iron
- fabric shears
- sewing machine and matching threads
- pins
- hand sewing needle

1 Cut out two side pieces for the house from the pale blue fabric, using the template on page 64, then cut two rectangles 7 x 8cm (2¾ x 3⅛in) for the front and back, and a square 7 x 7cm (2¾ x 2¾in) for the base, from the same fabric. Back the scraps with fusible web. Cut window and door shapes plus a decorative flower piece from the appliqué fabric. Cut three rectangles 9 x 7cm (3½ x 2¾in) from the blue gingham fabric for the roof and needlecase.

2 Iron the appliqué pieces on to the back, front and sides of the house. Machine sew around all the pieces in matching thread.

3 Place the front and one of the side pieces of the house right sides together, pin and then machine sew them together. Do the same for the other side piece and then the back piece, which will need to be sewn along both edges.

4 While the house is inside out, pin one of the roof pieces in place along the sloping edge of the roof, right sides together and machine sew. Stitch all of the remaining edges of the roof in the same way.

5 To make the needlecase that goes on the roof, pin the other two gingham pieces together and machine sew around one short side and the two long sides. Turn the case the right way out then pin and machine sew the final edge. Carry on the machine stitching all around the edge of the rectangle to give a unified look.

6 With the house still inside out, pin the square base into position. Machine sew around three sides. Turn the right way out.

7 To attach the needlecase, fold the piece in half widthways and pin on to the ridge of the roof. Carefully machine sew where pinned.

8 Firmly stuff the whole piece with toy stuffing through the gap left at the base, then hand sew to close.

Templates

Union Jack Pillow, page 22

Once you have drawn round the pieces, flip them over to create the other side of the flag. Draw and cut round the cross as one piece.

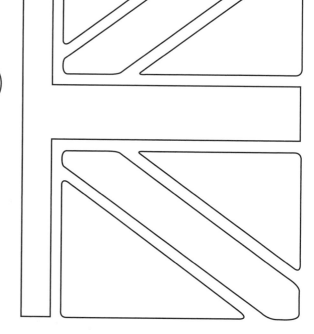

Mini Monster, page 20

Hedgehog, page 28, base

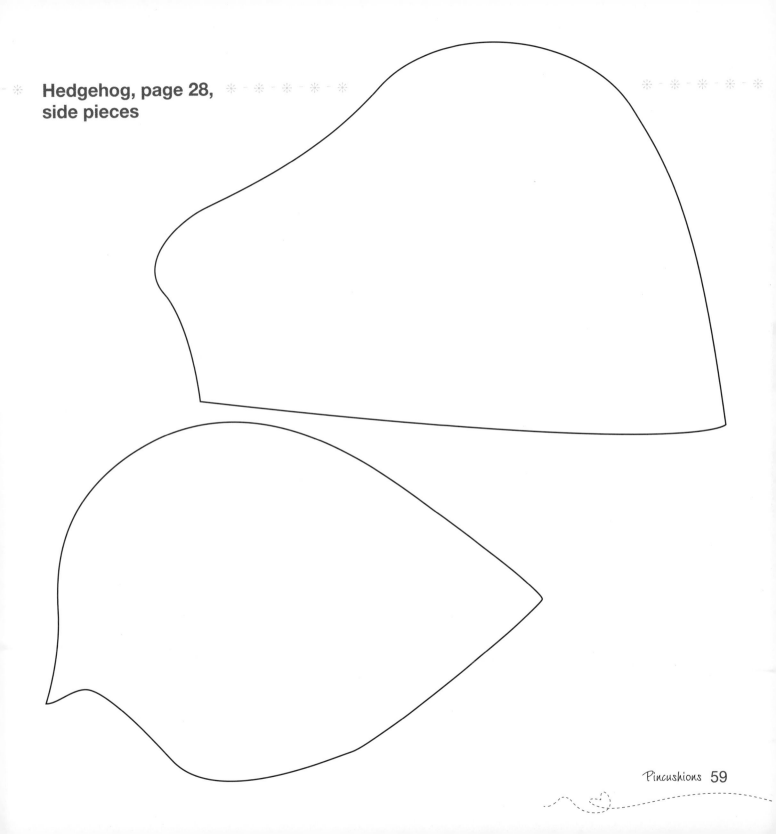

**Hedgehog, page 28,
side pieces**

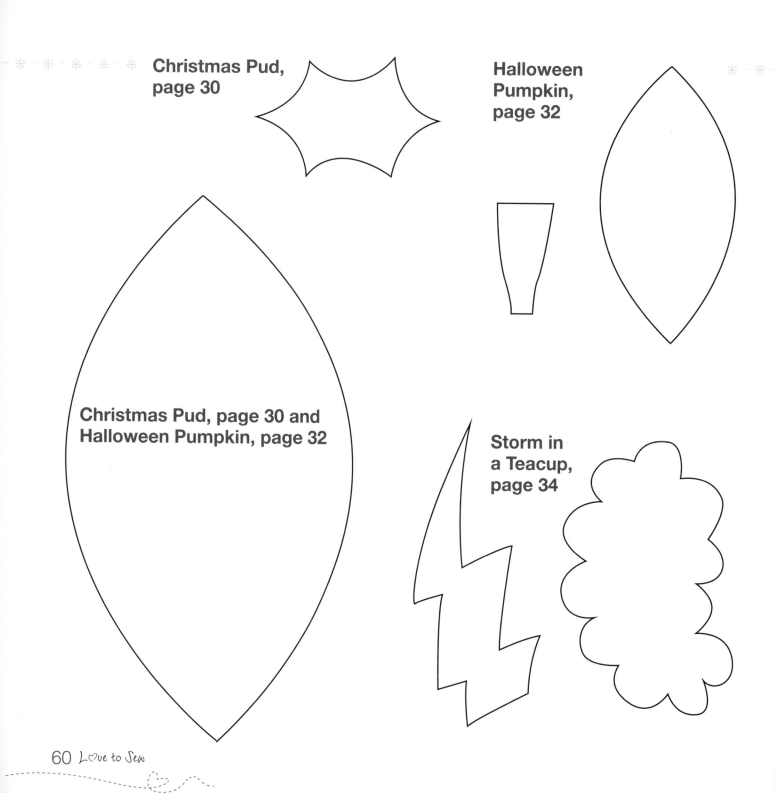

**Christmas Pud,
page 30**

**Halloween
Pumpkin,
page 32**

**Christmas Pud, page 30 and
Halloween Pumpkin, page 32**

**Storm in
a Teacup,
page 34**

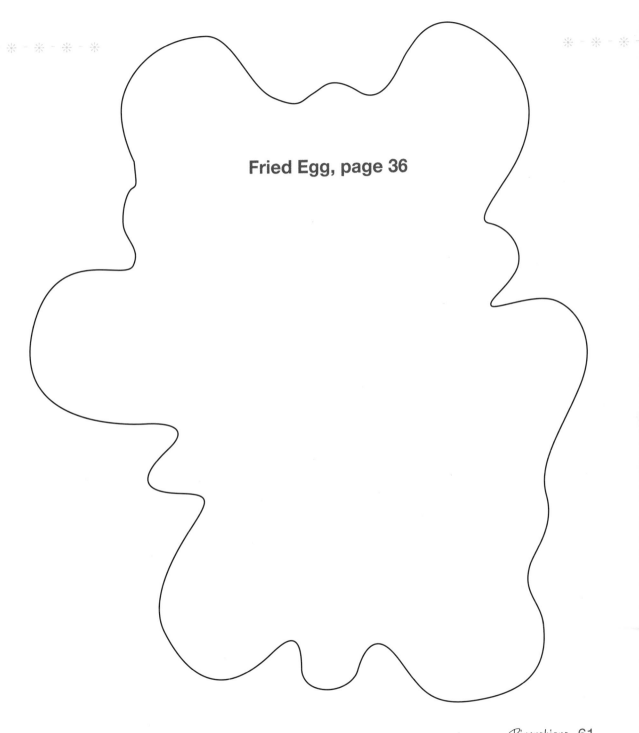

Fried Egg, page 36

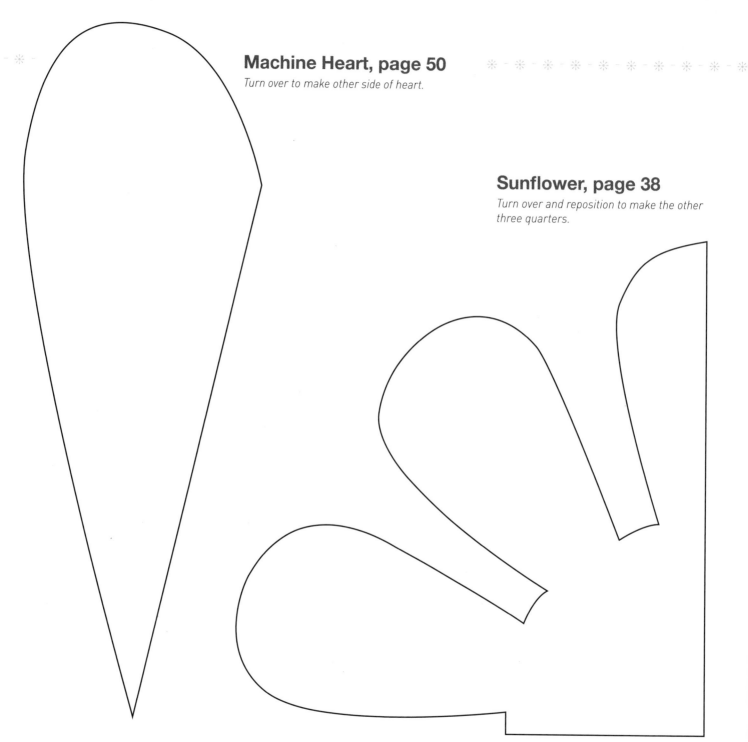

Machine Heart, page 50

Turn over to make other side of heart.

Sunflower, page 38

Turn over and reposition to make the other three quarters.

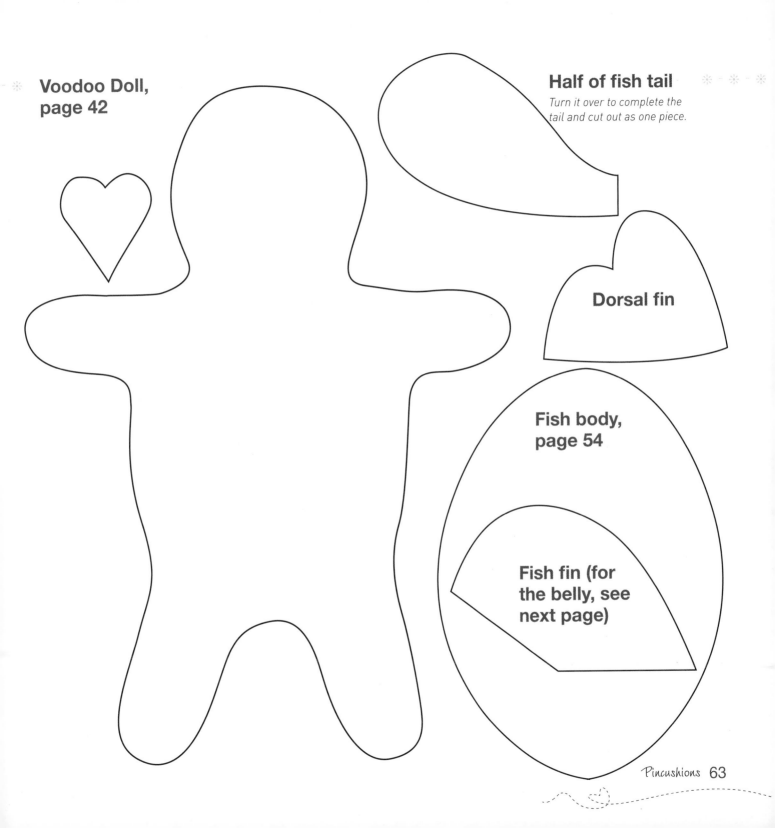

Voodoo Doll,
page 42

Half of fish tail
Turn it over to complete the tail and cut out as one piece.

Dorsal fin

Fish body,
page 54

Fish fin (for the belly, see next page)

Fish belly, page 54

Flat Cat, page 44

House, page 56

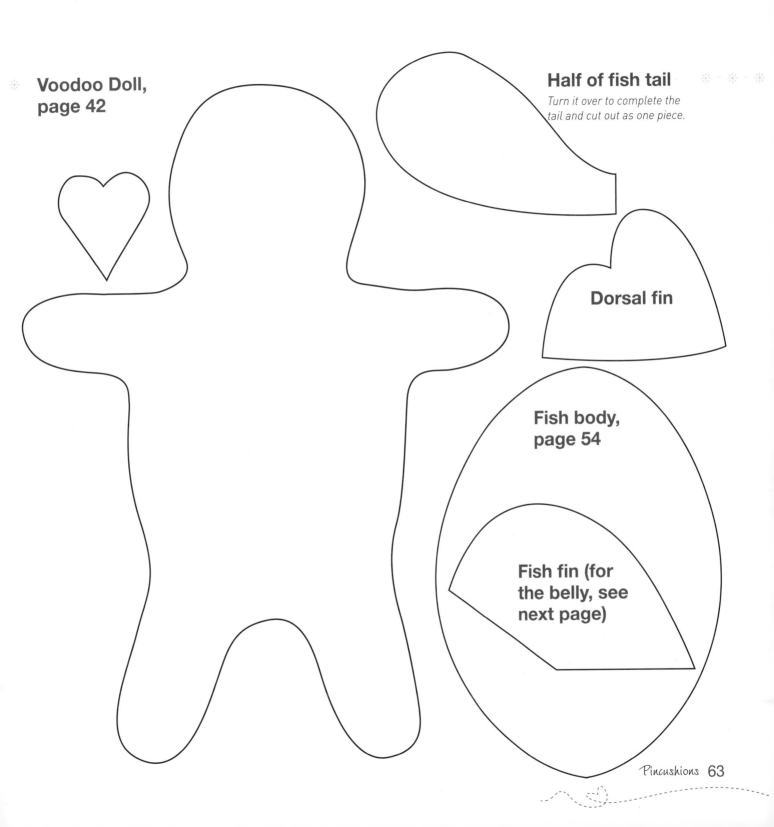

**Voodoo Doll,
page 42**

Half of fish tail
*Turn it over to complete the
tail and cut out as one piece.*

Dorsal fin

**Fish body,
page 54**

**Fish fin (for
the belly, see
next page)**

Fish belly, page 54

Flat Cat, page 44

House, page 56